Let's Play Tag!

- Read the Page
- Read the Story
- Repeat
- Stop
- Game
- Yes
- No

TO USE THIS BOOK WITH THE TAG™ READER you must download audio from the LeapFrog Connect application.
The LeapFrog Connect application can be installed from the CD provided with your Tag Reader or at leapfrog.com/tag.

For everyone who's ever felt
misjudged or misunderstood

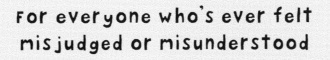

Walter the Farting Dog Goes on a Cruise

William Kotzwinkle, Glenn Murray, and Elizabeth Gundy

illustrated by Audrey Colman

"Look at the size of that ship!" said Billy.

"It's as high as a twenty-three-story building," said Father.

"It has everything in it," said Mother. "Even a shopping mall."

"And five swimming pools," said Betty.

Walter farted excitedly.

"Welcome aboard," said the Cruise Director.
"What a nice dog," said Pet Officer Smedley.
The ship pulled away from the dock.

The horn sounded.
Walter farted.

"All our animal friends stay down here in the Pet Palace," said Pet Officer Smedley. "We do our best to make them completely comfortable."

Walter sniffed around the fancy room.

"I'm off for my first round of golf," said Father.

"I'm off for my massage," said Mother.

"We're off to swim in all five pools," said Billy.

"Don't worry, Walter," added Betty, "we'll be back in a little while."

Walter settled down on a plush cushion. *Not bad*, he said to himself, and farted.

As soon as the door of the Pet Palace closed, trouble started brewing. Dogs began growling. Cats began hissing. Birds began squawking.

Why?

Walter was farting.

"Get that stinker out of here!" said the parrot in the corner.

Pet Officer Smedley returned with some pet treats and was instantly enveloped in a fart-cloud.

"This smells like an emergency to me," he said, and opened all the vents.

9

On the golf course, Father was lining up a putt when he noticed a familiar smell.

"What's that horrible odor?" said one of the other golfers.

"Must be the sea air," said Father.

But Father knew it wasn't the sea air. He saw Pet Officer Smedley coming toward him.

"We've got a problem with that dog of yours," said Smedley.

Father, Mother, Betty, and Billy were led back to the Pet Palace.

"Fart alert! Fart alert!" squawked the parrot.

"We're going to have to put Walter in quarantine," said Smedley.

Oh no, thought Walter.

"Lower the lifeboats! Lower the lifeboats!" squawked the parrot. "Women and parrots first!"

They decided to put Walter in the room where they stored the stinky cheeses.

"Don't worry, Walter," said Billy, "we won't be far away."

"We'll visit you a whole lot," said Betty as she closed the door.

Fair enough, thought Walter, quietly farting.

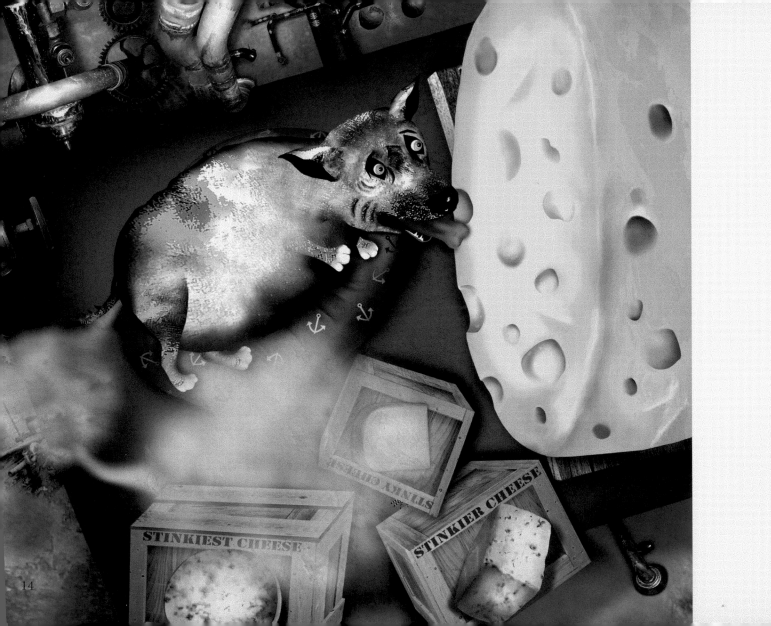

Among the stinky cheeses there was a big one that called to Walter.

I shouldn't eat that, thought Walter. *It doesn't belong to me. Yet here we are together. Me and the cheese.*

Perhaps if I just licked it lightly, no one would notice.

He licked it lightly, then ate the entire cheese.

Even though Walter was tucked away deep in the belly of the ship, his farts crept out under the door, slithered along the hallway, and made their way upstairs. By the next day, all six dining rooms were filled with farts and angry passengers.

"This ship stinks!"

"We want our money back!"
"Please be patient, ladies and gentlemen," said the cruise Director.
"We're having a little problem with the ventilation system, but we'll
have it under control in a few minutes."

The captain said, "Put that dog overboard."

Walter was lowered in a lifeboat, which was tied to the back of the ship.

"This will be fun, Walter," said Billy.

"Officer Smedley promised he would bring you treats every day," said Betty.

Fair enough, thought Walter, farting.

That night, the huge block of cheese inside him began doing its work, plugging up all the farts.

The passengers were enjoying themselves again, while Walter trailed behind in his lonely lifeboat.

The gas is building badly, he said, *but at least I'm still attached to the ship.*

Suddenly, the computer system that controlled everything on the ship crashed, and the backup system crashed right behind it. The power died, the engines quit, and the ship drifted helplessly. Everybody grew hot and cranky.

In his lifeboat, Walter was having his own problems. The gas pains were unbearable.

Try not to think about it, he said to himself. Twisting to look at his tail, he realized, *If that cheese lets go, I'll be blown halfway to the Arctic circle.*

He felt the gas bubble building...and building...and building...

He dug in with his paws and braced himself.

If anything breaks my perfect concentration, I'm done for.

A fly landed on his nose.

He looked at the fly.

The fly looked at him.

There was a deep rumble as the cheese shifted inside him.

A few small farts came out and gently pushed the lifeboat up against the ship. *That wasn't so bad*, said Walter.

But then all the farts that had been blocked for days came out with the roar of a rocket.

The ship heaved forward. Walter hung on, still farting.

"Warp speed!" squawked the parrot in the Pet Palace.

"We must be back to full power," said Father, gripping the deck rail. But it was much more than full power. It was fart power. It shot the ship over the horizon and into port.

"Right on time," said the captain.

When the cruise was over, Pet Officer Smedley presented Walter with a sailor hat.

"It was an honor having Walter on our cruise."

"We had a great time, but it's good to be back on land," said Mother.

"Anyone for pizza?" asked Father.

"Hold the cheese!" squawked the parrot.

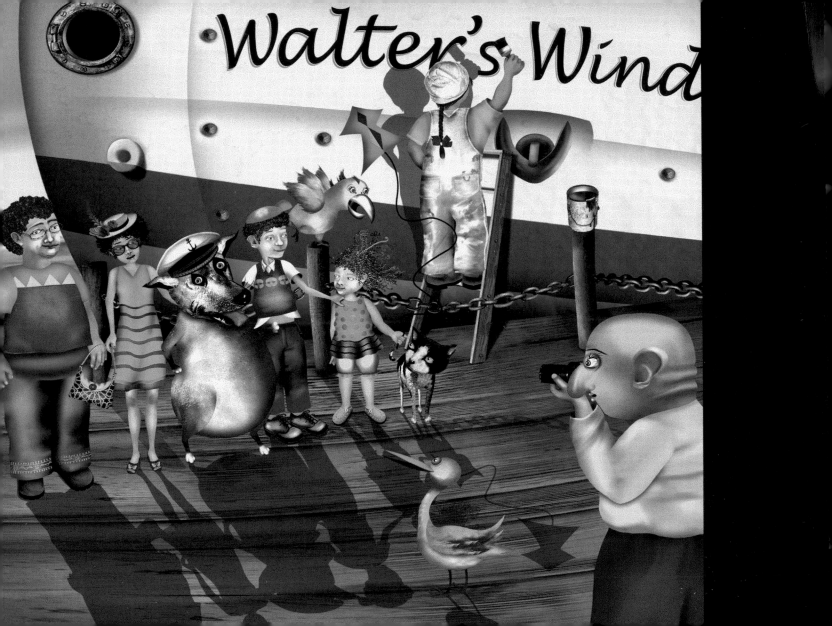